Elephant Rescue

Contents

Baby elephants   2
Helping baby elephants   4
A new family   6
Feeding time   8
Play time   10
Bath time   12
Bed time   14
Growing up   16
Back to the wild   18
Coming back   20
Glossary and index   21
Life in a rescue centre   22

Written by Louise Spilsbury

Baby elephants

A baby elephant is called a calf. When a calf is born, it's already about one metre tall! It can stand up soon after it's born and after a day or two, it can walk and follow its mother.

In the wild, a baby elephant lives with a **herd** of female elephants. The calf's mother, sisters, aunties and grandmothers all help to take care of it. They help to feed it and protect it from danger.

Helping baby elephants

Some people kill adult elephants and sell the animals' meat or **tusks**. Up to 36,000 adult elephants are **poached** every year. The baby elephants left behind can't take care of themselves.

In countries where elephants live, such as Kenya, India and Thailand, there are elephant rescue centres. These are based near elephant **habitats** so rescue teams can find and collect **orphan** elephants as soon as someone reports seeing one.

a rescue team taking an orphan elephant to the rescue centre

A new family

At the rescue centre, **keepers** take care of the orphan calves. Some calves miss their mothers and their herd so much that they die, so keepers give the new calves lots of love and attention.

In the wild, a calf has many carers. At the rescue centre, each calf has several keepers. This is important because if a calf becomes too fond of one of its keepers, it might die if that keeper leaves.

Feeding time

An elephant calf usually drinks milk from its mother's body. Keepers feed the calves a special type of milk from huge bottles. Calves drink ten litres of milk a day during their first year!

Keepers encourage nervous new calves to take milk by feeding them from behind a big blanket. This reminds the calf of snuggling into its mother's body and makes it feel safe.

Play time

In the wild, elephant calves walk about 15 to 20 kilometres with their herd each day. They also play with other elephants in the herd. This helps them to get to know the other elephants and grow strong.

two elephant calves playing together with an old tree trunk

At the rescue centre, keepers take calves for long walks, too. The calves play with each other and with the keepers. They push, pull and chase each other and they play with balls and other toys.

Bath time

Keepers take elephants to splash about in pools of water to keep them cool. The calves roll in mud, too. A mud layer helps to stop the sun burning their skin and it stops insects biting them.

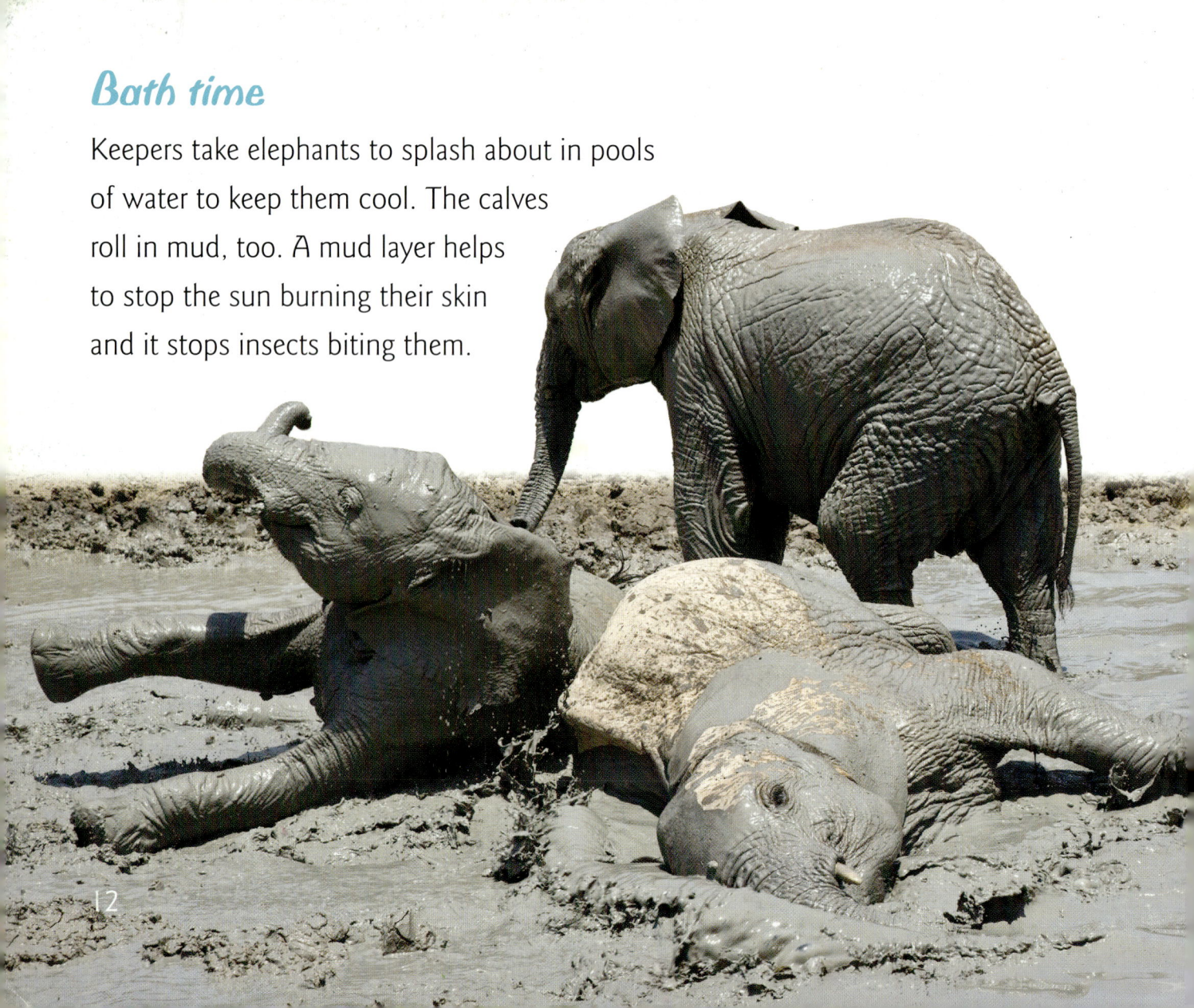

In the wild, a baby elephant's mother shelters it from the harsh sun with her huge body. Keepers carry an umbrella over younger calves and rub sun cream into their ears to prevent sunburn.

rubbing sun cream onto a calf

Bed time

In the wild, an elephant calf sleeps close to its mother all night. This keeps it warm and makes it feel safe.

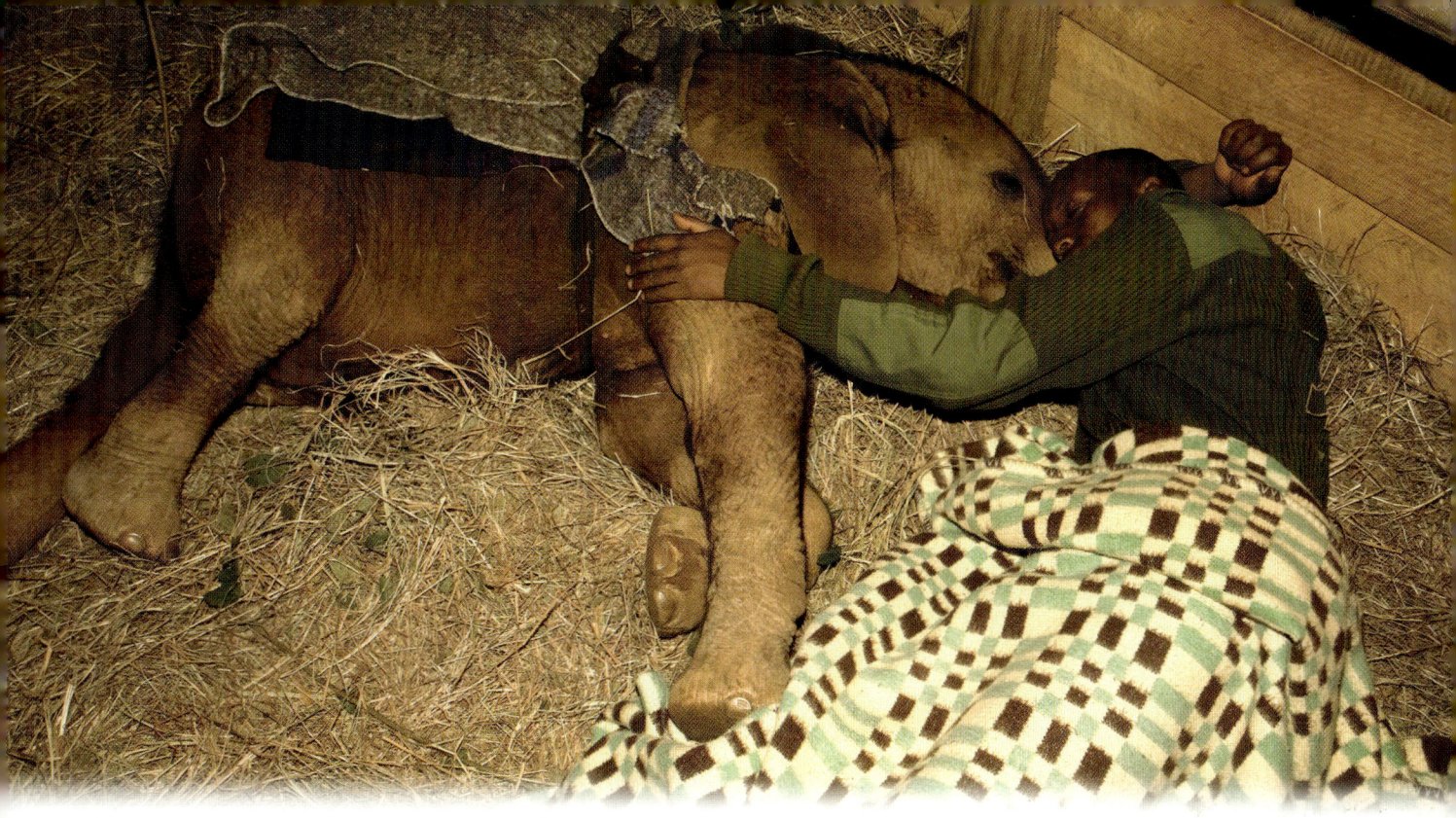

At the rescue centre, keepers wrap calves in blankets and sleep in a bed next to them. Young calves feed every three hours in the day and in the night. Keepers have to wake up every three hours at night to feed the calves a bottle of milk!

Growing up

When calves are two, keepers move them to a **national park** where older orphan elephants live safely in the wild. In the day, calves mix with these wild elephants. They learn to use their **trunks** to get and eat plants.

At night, keepers take calves home to feed them milk and keep them safe. Calves get hungry and scared if they stay out all night.

Back to the wild

Calves choose when to live in the wild all the time. They return to their keepers at night until they are about four to drink milk. After that, they start to stay out at night.

Gradually, most calves feel braver and safer, and choose to stay with the wild herd all the time. Some calves are more nervous and are eight or ten years old before they leave!

This calf has returned for food.

elephants returning to their keepers

Coming back

Elephants never forget! They sometimes come back to the rescue centre to visit their family of keepers. Some come for help when they're hungry or hurt. Some come to show keepers when they have a calf of their own!

Glossary

habitats   natural homes for animals or plants

herd   group of elephants

keepers   people who care for an animal

national park   a special area of land that is protected from poachers

orphan   child whose parents are dead

poached   killed animals illegally

trunks   the long noses of elephants

tusks   special, long teeth

Index

calf   2, 3, 6, 8, 9, 14, 20

calves   6, 8, 9, 10, 11, 12, 13, 14, 15, 16, 18,

ears   13

herd   3, 6, 10, 18

keepers   6, 8, 9, 11, 12, 13, 14, 15, 16, 18, 20

milk   8, 9, 15, 16, 18

mother   2, 3, 6, 8, 9, 13, 14

orphan   5, 6, 16

trunks   16

tusks   4

wild   3, 6, 10, 13, 14, 16, 18

Life in a rescue centre

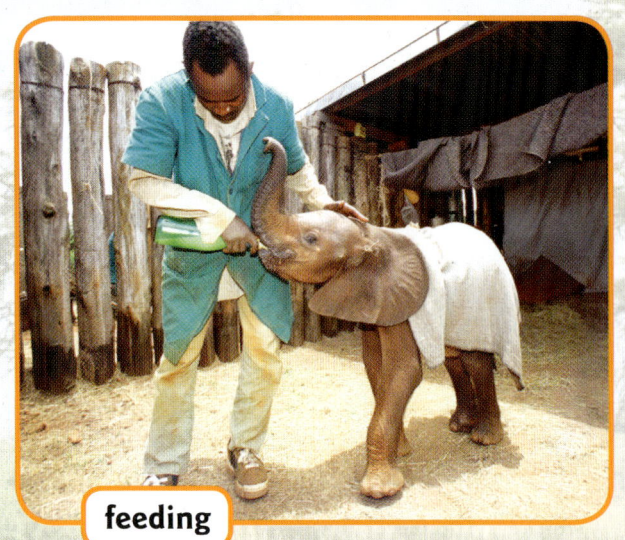
feeding

walking

playing

rolling in mud

sleeping

learning

Ideas for reading

Written by Gillian Howell
Primary Literacy Consultant

Learning objectives: (*reading objectives correspond with Purple band; all other objectives correspond with Copper band*) read independently and with increasing fluency longer and less familiar texts; identify and make notes of the main points of section(s) of text; sustain conversation, explain or give reasons for their views or choices; write non-narrative texts using structures of different text-types
Curriculum links: Citizenship, Geography
Interest words: elephant, rescue, calf, danger, poached, Thailand, orphan
Resources: internet, ICT
Word count: 695

Getting started

- Read the title on the front cover together and discuss the picture. Ask the children what sort of elephant this is, e.g. a baby elephant, and what is happening to it. Ask them to speculate about the sort of information they will find in the book.

- Turn to the back cover and read the blurb together to confirm the children's ideas about the content. Ask them to suggest reasons why some elephants need rescuing.

- Turn to the contents. Ask the children if they think it will make any difference to the information if they read chapters in sequence or dip in to particular chapters that interest them first.

Reading and responding

- Read together to pp4–5 and discuss whether the children's first ideas about why elephants need rescuing were correct. Encourage them to give a personal opinion about elephant poaching and ensure they are able to read the word *poach*.

- Ask the children to read the book quietly. Ask them to make notes of why baby orphan elephants need to be helped and how this is done at the rescue centre. Listen to the children and prompt as necessary.

- As they read, pause occasionally and ask them what added information or effect the photographs bring to the book, e.g. on pp6–7 ask what the photographs tell them about the elephants and their keepers, and how the photos make them feel.